Witchcraft Supplies

A Guide for Solitary Beginner Practitioners to the Tools a Witch Needs for Her Rituals and Spells

Table of Contents

Introduction 1
Chapter 1: The Basics 5
    Altars and Common Altar Tools 5
    Herbs, Stones, and Crystals 9
    Charging and Cleansing Your Tools 12
    Correspondence Charts 17
    Grimoires and Books of Shadows 19
Chapter 2: Getting Crafty 23
    The Benefits of DIY Supplies 23
    A Brief History of Household Witchery 25
    Spell Bags 28
    Mirror Boxes 32
    Witch Jars 34
Chapter 3: Tools by Spell Type 40
    Love Spells 40
    Moon Spells 42
    Nature Spells 45
    City Spells 48
    Adapting Tools for Your Spell 51
Chapter 4: Divination as a Tool 54
    Oracle and Tarot Cards 55
    Scrying in Water, Flame, and Smoke 61
    Pendulums 66
    Modern Divination Practices 72

Dreams 80

Portents and Omens 83

Chapter 5: Meditation and Visualization as a Tool 86

Grounding 86

Centering 91

Meditation and Visualization in Spellwork and Magic 99

Shadow Work 102

Conclusion 108

Introduction

Thank you for purchasing *Witchcraft Supplies: A Guide for Solitary Practitioners to the Tools a Witch Needs for Her Rituals and Spells*. This book was a complete labor of love and it means so much to me that I can share my words with you.

The tools of witchcraft are many and varied. They are often as unique as the witch that wields them. Indeed, the form of witchcraft your practice may affect how you wield your tools and what sort of tools you gravitate toward. For a more in-depth look at the different kind of witches, I suggest my books *The Beginner Witch* or *Modern Witchcraft for Beginners*. Both go into a fair amount of detail on various types of witches and how to decide which label, if any, fits your practice.

While there are some tools that hold fast across all practices and spell types, others are specific to certain magical acts. This book will help you select the best tools for the job you need to do. And, more than that, it will teach you how to properly care for those tools as well as how to adapt the tools you have for the spell you want to cast.

Before we move into the rest of the book, however, I want to take a moment to discuss what magic is. And, more importantly, what it is not. Magic in and of itself is a tool. It is not a miracle cure to any problem and magic alone cannot change your life. You need to support your magic with real-world, mundane action. These actions feed your magic with fresh energy and they are just as vital to your spells as the tools discussed within these pages.

And, to allay any fears some readers might have, magic is not evil. It is not selfish to a damaging degree. And it is not, in and of itself, a religious act. You can use magic without aligning yourself with any particular deity. On the same token, you can perform magic while aligned with very nearly any deity. It all comes down to what you are personally comfortable with as well as the rules of your religion, if you ascribe to one.

I also want to make it clear that the spells in this book are written for general magic practitioners. Many people falsely believe that Wiccans and witches are the same thing. And while many Wiccans are witches, not all witches are Wiccan. Wiccan magic users are bound by the rules of Wicca and, more importantly, the Wiccan Rede. These guidelines affect how they perform their magic as well as what magical acts they can perform and what tools that can use.

While many of the tools in this book may be familiar to Wiccans who pick up this book, I am approaching these tools in as broad a manner as possible while still being helpful. Magic is for everyone, regardless of religious affiliation, ethnicity, or heritage. Magic is a personal and intimate expression of your own internal power. And, for that reason, this book is written so that all witches regardless of the specifics of their practice, can apply the information within these pages.

Chapter 1: The Basics

Although this book is all about exploring a wide range of tools, certain tools are popular in depictions of witches for a reason. The tools we go over in this chapter are among the most common, regardless of a witch's religious affiliation or specific practice. Some of the items are called by specific names, depending on the rules of a person's specific practice. For the sake of clarity, I have chosen to use generic names for all of the tools. I will, however, mention common alternative names when I discuss a tool that has one.

Altars and Common Altar Tools

The most common tool among witches is not the wand. It is, in fact, the altar. Most witches – although certainly not all – practice their magic in tandem with some form of religion. And that religion is not always Wicca. There are Pagan witches of all stripes as well as Christian witches, Fae witches, and witches who feel the magic itself is a religion in addition to secular witches who do not practice any sort of religion with their magic.

Altars are essential among those witches for whom magic is a part of their religious practice. These spaces are not only a main worship point for the deity or deities that the witch worships. They also serve as a place for the witch to cast most of her spells. It is where she houses her tools when they are not in use and it may even be where she creates her handmade magical tools, depending on the size of her altar and the type of tool she is making.

A witch's altar can come in many forms. Some witches prefer to create their altars on wall-mounted shelves. Others opt for whole tables dedicated to magical and religious purposes. Of course, both options work best for witches who are "out" and very open about their practice with anyone who may walk into their home. Not all witches fit this description. And, as such, their altars are often very different.

Witches who want a more discreet altar may opt for a miniature one, usually built inside of a box. Some are even the size of a mint tin and intended to serve only as a focal point for the witch's power during spells or as a place for her to commune with her deities.

Others might use a table that they can take apart, such as the kind sold at most hardware stores. They store this table, in pieces, under their bed or in a closet. Their tools and altar decorations are stored in another box or scattered around their room, used as décor until they need to put them to magical use. When that time comes, the witch assembled her table and sets up her altar. Although this option is quite a bit of work, it does provide a little more energy to the spell or ritual, since the witch expended the energy necessary to set everything up and then take everything down when she was done.

Yet another altar option is a digital altar. This modern take on the witch's altar can only serve as a focal point and a place to commune with deities or spirits, of course. But there are many modern witches who keep blogs that serve as a form of altar. Or they create static images that they change and update when other witches would change the décor on their altar. Their tolls are typically stored near to the computer where the witch keeps her digital altar and brought out when it is time to work magic. I explore the idea of digital altars, as well as many other ways that magic and technology can support one another, in my book *Modern Witchcraft for Beginners*. And, as I say in that book as well, each witch must find the altar that best suits her needs, both religious and mundane.

You now have the groundwork of what makes a good altar. It is not so much the material it is made from but rather how well it serves your magical and religious practice. But what about the tools that go on your altar or the decorations I mentioned earlier? Both of these topics might seem a bit confusing to new witches. Rest assured, we will cover them both together.

As a witch's altar is a personal reflection of her practice, the exact tools and decorations will vary. But witches usually have a ritual knife of some kind or a wand, both of which are used to help direct the flow of the witch's energy. These knives or wands – as, for the purpose of directing her energy, a witch could use either – can be made of any material. Some witches choose to make their own while others prefer store-bought.

Many practitioners also keep a chalice or cauldron on their altar to hold water. In certain magical practices, such as Wicca, the chalice represents the female divine and the water within represents the life source from which we all emerge. Other practices, however, use the chalice strictly as a drinking vessel so that the witch can toast or cheer the spirits and deities she works with or worships.

Even more common are incense and candles. Both come in a wide variety of scents and candles come in a wide range of colors so that witches can customize both the scent and the appearance of their altar. If the witch in question worships nature, candles and incense can represent fire or air, thanks to the flame or the ember that each carries. They can also provide a focal point for the witch when she is meditating or working through a breathing exercise, such as those I describe in my book, *The Beginner Witch*.

Decorations are a little trickier. Some witches ascribe to the Wiccan Wheel of the Year and decorate their altar according to the season and the nearest religious holiday on the Wheel. Others arrange and decorate their altars to honor specific religious figures or spirits. For these witches, the seasons are not so much a call to change the appearance of their altar but a reminder to keep it fresh and clean. And then there are witches who do not decorate their altar at all. They forego flowers, stones, images, or growing things in favor of keeping a clean work surface. As with choosing the best type of altar, each witch must choose how to decorate her altar. Or whether she wants to decorate it at all.

Herbs, Stones, and Crystals

Another popular tool among magic users are herbs, stones, and crystals. I cannot go into as much depth on all of these topics as I would really like. That is a whole other book in and of itself. But there are some basics that every witch should know before she starts working with these materials.

The very first rule – and the one rule that no witch should ever forget – is to do your research. There are many books out there that suggest eating herbs or certain combination of herbs. And there are books that say you should cleanse all of your stones by leaving them in water overnight. And, most of the time, these suggestions are fine. Or, at the very least, they are harmless.

But that is not always the case. I have stumbled across spells suggesting that a witch can use belladonna in her tea and that they can cleanse their selenite stones in water overnight. Neither suggestion is true. And, in the case of the belladonna tea, it is deadly. Belladonna is also known as Deadly Nightshade and is incredibly toxic. Selenite will dissolve in water. And if it does not dissolve completely, it will be severely damaged. Thankfully I had done my research prior to stumbling on these suggestions. Otherwise, I would have ended up with a damaged stone, a trip to the ER, or worse.

Always, *always*, do your own research before ingesting anything or submerging anything in water. And if a spell suggests that you submerge crystals in water and then *drink* the water – an increasingly popular trend – you should take even more time doing your research before you follow the suggestion. This is especially true if you take any kind of medication. Certain herbs can have terrible interactions with medications. Or, barring an interaction, they may render your medication ineffective. When in doubt, ask a doctor before ingesting any new herbs.

Once you have done your research and you know it is safe to incorporate herbs and stones into your practice, the next step is finding a reputable source to get them from. Natural food stores – and an increasing number of grocery stores – have bulk spice sections. These are wonderful options if your spell calls for the herb in a general sense. If you have to find a fresh version of the herb, your best bet is a nursery or gardening center.

Finding reputable stone dealers is quite a different matter. Many magic supply shops – often called metaphysical shops – sell stones and crystals. And though most vendors will not willfully deceive their customers, there is quite a bit of misinformation out there and not all shopkeeps are experts in every item they stock.

Quartz is an excellent example of this. The stone and all its variants are wildly popular in the magical community, to the point where even witches who do not generally use stones will turn to quartz for their spells. Despite its popularity, however, not many people know that quartz is naturally colorless. Or that "rainbow quartz" is not a naturally occurring stone but rather mad-made one created by bonding a thin metal layer on top of clear quartz. Quartz is also often dyed to create more vivid colors than its colored variants are going to natural produce.

To some witches, none of this matters. They choose their stones based on the way the stone feels to them, rather than based on what others say the stones should mean. But there are many witches who follow the suggestions of others and are completely unaware of what it is they are using. As with herbs, doing a little bit of research will make sure you are getting the stone you want and not an alternative.

Of course, knowing about the stones in front of you is only part of the decision when you want to involve stone or crystals in your practice. You have to know which crystals are right for your spell or your practice in general. Sometimes this information can be learned from researching where the stone came from and what it is made of. At other times you will want to reference a correspondence chart, which I will discuss later in this chapter.

Charging and Cleansing Your Tools

Once you have your tools selected, you need to know how to take care of them. When it comes to magic, this usually takes the form of cleansing and charging them. Cleansing is the term for any process through which you remove negative, stale, or otherwise unwanted energy from anything. It is usually applied to magical tools, as it is here, but you could also cleanse your living space, car, clothing, or mundane belongings. Charging, on the other hand, is when you fill an object with a certain kind of energy that you want it to have. As with cleansing, this usually refers to the tools you use in your craft. But you can charge just about anything if you know the process well enough.

There are several ways to cleanse your tools. The five most common are moonlight, sunlight, smoke, water, and salt. Each one has its benefits and drawbacks, as I will outline below. Although you can use these approaches one at a time, some witches find that particularly stubborn energy requires multiple cleansings or several forms of cleansing all at once before it will let go of an object. Always try one cleansing method and see how it works before you opt for multiple cleansing approaches or periods of cleansing.

Moonlight is the most popular cleansing option. You can cleanse anything in moonlight without fear of damaging the item or causing an odd reaction. And as long as you can find a patch of moonlight big enough for the item, you can cleanse it. The real downside comes with timing. You can only cleanse things under the full moon or the new moon. There are spells that allow you to use the energy of the waning moon to cleanse something, but that can take a week or more. So you either cleanse for a long period of time or you can only cleanse your items on certain days of the months.

Sunlight is a common alternative. The sun's energy is considered hotter than the moon's and, since the sun burns roughly the same route every day, you can cleanse any time you want. The drawback to sun cleansing, however, is that doing it too often – or leaving your tools in the sun – can cause the coloring to fade. This is especially true for paper products such as your grimoire and certain stones like rose quartz. Over time, the sunlight will fade their color. And in the case of rose quartz, it may render the stone utterly colorless. If you do choose to cleanse your tools in the sun, try to limit how often you do so and take care with how you store the items between cleansing days.

Smoke is another popular option. Most Neo-Pagans and witches use white sage, but there are a few issues with this. The first is that white safe is sacred to certain Native American groups and the rate at which it is being used by non-Natives has created shortages several times over the last few years. The other problem is that many companies that sell white sage "smudging" bundles misuse the term and overharvest the sage under questionable growing conditions, further adding to shortages.

There are ways to ethically buy white sage, of course. Many Native-owned companies grow their sage with safe, organic methods and harvest it at sustainable levels. Buying from these companies not only supports Natives who have long used white sage but also their practices which help prevent shortages and damage to the land.

If you do not want to use white sage at all, there are several alternatives. You can create an ember on the end of a cedar stick and cleanse your tools with its smoke. You can also use a variety of incense or burn fresh herbs from your garden in a cauldron. There are many herbs that can be used for cleansing and protection. To find them, you need only look up correspondence charts online or, as I outline in the next section, you can create your own based on your relationship with plants and herbs you have access to.

Water is one of the most intuitive cleansing options out there. But, as I mentioned in the Herbs, Stones, and Crystals section, it might not work for all items. Some stones do not react well to water, plant material will likely rot, and water obviously does not work well with paper products. Although this discounts many tools, there are still ways you can use water to cleanse magical objects.

Some witches choose to charge water under the light of the moon and then use this Moon Water to cleanse their objects by misting them with it, or wiping them down. You can also add a bit of moon water to your washing machine to help cleanse your clothes or any fabric you use your altar that is machine washable. Barring the use of Moon Water, some objects can be immersed in water in order to cleanse them. Just be sure you know how the object will interact with water and be sure you don't unintentionally rust or disintegrate something. Or, as is the case with some stones, release toxic fumes.

Salt is the last common option when a witch needs to cleanse something. Typically this involves the object being placed in a container just slightly bigger than itself and then completely covered with salt. The salt then draws out the unwanted energy and, when it is composted, returns that energy to the earth so it can be cleansed and returned to the universe for future use. This can be a little pricy, depending on how much salt is needed. And it does not work well with certain stones or metals. But it can be helpful if you need to cleanse something in a pinch.

Compared to cleansing your tools, charging them is a very simple process. You can either leave them in moonlight to absorb the moon's energy, as is the case with Moon Water. Or you can set them on your altar to take on the energy you seek. You can also actively feed energy into an object, but that is more along the lines of enchanting something than charging it. Charging is a more indirect action and typically creates a more thorough bond between the item and the energy it is taking on.

With both charging methods, the key is to set your intention. When you set the item out, whether in moonlight or on your altar, you need to state what it is you want to see happen. Simply setting it out does not direct the energies around you and it does not let the higher power you work with understand that you need something from them. Charging something is a very passive kind of spell. And, as I discuss in my book *Modern Witchcraft for Beginners*, intention is everything when it comes to spellwork.

If you use these two methods, you will be well on your way to properly caring for your magical tools. You will also want to keep them free of mundane grime, of course. But, generally speaking, it is the psychic grime that you will have to clean off most often. And with these techniques close at hand, doing so will quickly become second nature.

Correspondence Charts

Magical correspondence charts are tricky things. For a long time, they were taken as hard and fast rules. Green was for prosperity, lavender was only used for sleep spells, and you could not cast a spell to find love without a chunk of rose quartz. But a shift has taken place over the last few decades. And as the conversation around modern magic grew to include witches from all backgrounds and from all over the world, the idea of a single unified correspondence chart began to fade.

You can still find correspondence charts online. There are countless charts that give you the connections between everything from planets to herbs to stones to colors to days of the week. Every deity in a major European pantheon has had a correspondence chart created in their name so that devotees and magic workers could more easily connect with the divine being of their choice. And there is, by and large, nothing wrong with using these charts.

But when you use a premade correspondence chart, you want to be sure and engage your sense of discernment. I cover discernment more fully in my book *The Beginner Witch*. But, at its core, discernment simply means looking critically at the information in front of you. And it is a habit all witches need. If you find a chart that says you have to have a hard to find herb in order to cast a spell, there is a good chance that the spell was not written with people from your part of the planet in mind. Or, barring that, it was written with a very specific myth or legend in mind, ease of access for the ingredients notwithstanding.

Premade correspondence charts are helpful. But that does not mean that you cannot make your own. In fact, as you become more comfortable working within your magical practice, it is a very good idea for you to make your own correspondence charts. This task may seem daunting, even to the most experienced witch among us. But it is much less complicated than you might think.

To create your own correspondence chart, you need only look at the patterns found in your own spellwork. These patterns may include which spell ingredients work best for you, which days of the week seem to produce the strongest spells, what situations or locations boot your energy and which drain it, and which myths or legends stand out most clearly to you. All of these patterns can be tracked using your grimoire, as I will explain in the next section.

You can also create correspondence charts based on the type of magic you practice, the scientific properties of the ingredients you have in mind, or your own personal and cultural views. White, for example, symbolizes innocence, happiness, and new beginnings throughout much of Europe and North America. But in Japan and several other countries, white is the traditional color of funeral clothing. These cultural differences may change how white is used in spellwork by people from each location.

It will take time to make your own correspondence chart. Once you have one, however, you will find it much easier to adapt spells you find online and to write your own spells. You can also add your chart to your grimoire as a personal reference for everything from divination to spellwork to dream interpretation.

Grimoires and Books of Shadows

You might not have heard of a grimoire. But if you consume popular media about witches, there is a good chance you have heard of a Book of Shadows. They are, in effect the same thing. Certain branches of magic users – namely Wiccans and Neo-Wiccans – simply prefer the term Book of Shadows over Grimoire. Both terms refer to a book where a witch records the spells she casts, their outcome, and any other magical actions she takes.

These books are usually depicted as huge leather-bound tomes filled with calligraphy and sumptuous illustrations. Grimoires do exist that fit this stereotype. But there are many other forms a grimoire can take. And the vast majority of grimoires you come across in your magical community will probably fall into the second category. A grimoire's primary use is not to be pretty, but to help you track the growth of your magical practice.

Some of the most effective grimoires are the simplest. A spiral notebook with "Grimoire" written across the front with a Sharpie. Or a three-ring binder full of loose leaf paper. These options are often less intimidating so witches feel more comfortable just writing down whatever comes to mind when they want to document their practice. If you have any concerns about "ruining" an expensive leather bound book or messing up when you try to create a Grimoire scrapbook, start with something a little more mundane.

Once you are comfortable creating a journal of your magic practice, you can go back and edit or rearrange your notes. These can then be transferred into the more aesthetically pleasing grimoires that you see in films and on television. You might even find time to learn a bit of book binding so you can make your own. Without the pressure to get it right the first time, it is surprising what you might find to include in your grimoire if you decide on an "upgrade".

Like most everything in magic, Grimoires are intensely personal. You might start with one kind of grimoire and switch to another as time goes on. This does not mean you have to completely recreate your previous journals if you do not want to, of course. The change is a sign of your magical growth, in and of itself. It means that you have changed as a person and as a witch.

Grimoires are so variable and personal, in fact, that some witches forgo a physical book altogether. More and more often, modern witches are using their computers as their grimoires. This sometimes takes the form of a blog, much like an online altar can. And, for some witches, these blogs are one in the same. Other magic users keep a word document or PDF of their grimoire.

Digital journals are very easy to update and change when the need arises. They can also be sent to friends or fellow practitioners without losing control of the original, which is not possible with a physical book. Making copies in the event of a disaster is also a snap, as is printing the file out and turning it into a physical book. There are still some witches that do not think magic and technology should mix. But many modern witches are bucking that assumption every day. And their grimoires are quite the sight to behold.

Chapter 2: Getting Crafty

I say this a lot, but magic is an intensely personal practice. And though there are some magical tools you will have to buy in a store – unless you happen to be a metalworker and know of a good quartz deposit – making your own magical tools is a fantastic experience that every witch should have. DIY witchery has a very long history. Today, most supplies are store-bought. But there are a few that even the busiest witch will have to make herself.

This chapter will cover the benefits of making your own magical supplies as well as explaining a bit of the history behind DIY witchery. I've included a sample of an old spell that highlights what sort of crafty magic our foremothers engaged in. Finally, you will learn how to make a few key spell supplies that are not readily found in most stores.

The Benefits of DIY Supplies

Magic is fueled by two things: energy and intention. You usually set your intention by keeping the goal of your spell in mind while putting it together, and then again when you recite the incantation. Building energy into a spell, however, takes a little more legwork. Most of your magical energy with either come from your own energy stores or the energy of the higher power you choose to work with. But some can be added in before you raise a single protective ward. Making your own spell supplies is one such method.

When you make your own spell supplies, you are pouring a great deal of energy and intention into the work you do with your hands. Every time you pick up a supply for the DIY project, your thoughts will turn to the spell you have in mind. And if you are making the items for future spells that you have not quite decided on yet, you are still filling the crafted item with the intention to do magic. Your energy soaks into the materials every time you touch them. And when you pick the object up with a specific spell in mind, all of that intention and energy rises up, ready to do your bidding.

Making your own magical supplies also ties you more closely to your magical practice. Instead of spending a lot of time and money on something that was mass produced, you are creating something out of a vision in your mind using your own hands. This is essentially what magic does. It takes a vision in your mind and uses your energy to call it into reality. And while this may seem a little too on-the-nose, you have to remember that all energy in the universe is connected. When you create connections like this, it strengthens the web of your energy and builds up your magical works.

There are, of course, more mundane benefits to making your own spell supplies as well. When you make your own tools, you know exactly what is going into them. You can source materials from second hand shops or from items already found in your home. This gives you a level control over your magical tools that you simply do not have when someone else makes them. Sourcing your magical tools second hand also allows you to reduce your impact on the planet while saving a little bit of money. You just have to be sure that you cleanse the item before you use it in a spell, so that you do not carry any unwanted energy into the spell.

A Brief History of Household Witchery

It would be impossible to fit the entire history of DIY witchcraft into this book. This is in large part because, for much of history, all witchcraft was DIY witchcraft. Many early magic users did not have access to large shops where they could get anything they wanted. And they certainly did not have access to the internet where they could quite literally get anything if they had enough money. They might have gotten a few supplies from other people in their village or at the market. But for the most part, they gathered the supplies and made their tools themselves.

In some cases, these tools were things that were already lying around the house. The ceremonial knife – if they had one – was the best knife in the house. And the altar was probably a small side table that also honored the house and land spirits in addition to whatever gods were worshipped in the home. Witches grew their own herbs and traded with neighbors to get anything that they did not grow themselves.

Because of this, many of the earliest spells were very simple affairs that used everyday objects from around the house. This served the dual purpose of making it harder to spot a witch on sight, since witches and alleged witches have long been the targets of incredible violence. But even when magic workers were a common part of daily life, simple spells prevailed over highly ornate or rigidly structured rituals.

A spell was often a small item, the focused energy of the witch, and a prayer to whatever divine being or spirit the witch felt would best answer her request. That was it. One such spell that has come down through multiple families as a sort of folk belief is the button spell. To cast a button spell, one takes a loose button in their hand. They hold the button tight and focus all their energy and thoughts on the outcome they want or the type of thing they want to attract or repel. Then they say a prayer to a higher power and slip the button in their pocket. When the spell is no longer needed, they sew the button onto a garment, at which time it is released from its magical use.

This simple DIY spell can still be used today, though modern witches would recommend cleansing the button before you use it on a garment. And now that it is easier than ever to get our hands on crafting supplies, you can take your DIY work even further. Rather than stop at a single button, you can knit an entire garment and enchant it with a specific kind of energy, for example. There are even groups that already do something like this, in the form of prayer shawls and meditative knitting.

This project might seem a little daunting to newcomers, however. Particularly if you are not already familiar with fiber crafts. Thankfully, there are much simpler DIY projects that you can start with. The rest of this chapter is dedicated to three of the most common magical tools that a witch might have to make herself.

The first of these are spell bags. Many spells call for pouches or sachets that will hold herbs, crystals, and a variety of other materials in order to create a physical representation of the witch's spell. Personally, I find spell bags to be some of the easiest spells to cast. Buying new bags for every spell can get expensive. And finding the perfect bag can turn into more of a headache than the spell might be worth. But if you know how to make your own, a quick run to the fabric store for scrap fabric and twenty minutes of crafting means you have the perfect spell bag every time.

Mirror boxes are perfect for spells that range from protection spells to hexes, if you are partial to that sort of magic. They are easy to make and, thanks to the variety of materials you could use, easily customized to the specific spell you have in mind. And, finally, you will learn how to make a witch jar. Witch jars are more of a spell than a tool. But knowing how to make a variety of witch jars is an essential part of magic working. So this chapter will cover the basics and create the groundwork you need to put together your own custom witch jar with confidence.

Spell Bags

The term "spell bags" can refer to two things. The first is a simple cloth pouch that you intend to use in a spell. On the other hand "spell bag" can also refer to the same pouch after it has gone through the spell and now contains the contents of your magical working. In this section you will learn how to make the first kind of spell bag. If you are interested in making the second kind of spell bag, I encourage you to look into the spells contained within my other books.

If you are like me, sewing has never been your strong suit. I have bought so many books on sewing that I could start my own library. And yet it remains a mystery to me. Despite this, I regularly sew my own spell bags. They are one of the easiest sewing projects you can imagine and are easily customized for every spell, budget, and need.

Of course, there are fancier patterns out there. My pouches do not have a built-in drawstring, but are instead tied shut with a length of ribbon or cord. I actually prefer this method as it gives me a little more control over the spell as well as another way to customize my spell bag to my exact intention. That said, you may find yourself graduating from my design to a more complicated one over time.

But it is always best to start with the basics, as my family is fond of saying. And this bag is as basic as it can get. Before you start sewing, however, you have to decide what sort of material you want to use and how big you want it to be. Most of my completed spell bags fit comfortably in the palm of my hand. At their largest, they fit within both my hands. You can make the bag as big as you'd like, however. The pattern is very easy to scale up and down.

Choosing the material is a little trickier. For most spells, I use generic cotton fabric. Cotton is very common in North America and so it does not bring any real significance to my spell. If I am casting a love spell, however, I may opt for silk, lace, or velvet instead. These fabrics offer more sensation when touched and are often used in lingerie and other clothes associated with romance. For money spells, on the other hand, I might use brocade or linen. These fabrics are not only more costly but also more durable and fine to the touch.

In all of these examples, the fabric matches the intention of my spell. Once I have chosen the correct fabric for my spell bag, I select a specific color pattern that further aligns with the intention of my spell. When I do this, I refer to my personal correspondence chart, which I made just as I outlined earlier in this chapter. All of this works together to weave my magic into the project before I even get home from the fabric store.

Usually I only need to buy half a yard of fabric. And that is if I do not find a good match in the scrap fabric bins. Sometimes, if I need to make a large bag, I will search through table clothes and sheets at the thrift store, then choose from what I find there. It is often less expensive and prevents me from using new materials when there is already something in circulation that I can use.

Once I get the material home, if it is new, I quickly stitch a line around the entire outside edge of the fabric. This will prevent it from fraying when I put it in the wash. Then, regardless if it is new or used, I run the material through my washing machine with some other laundry. If it is new I try to run it through with black clothes or towels, in case the new material's dye runs at all.

When the material is dry, I iron it flat. Then I fold it in half – nice sides on the inside – so that, when I cut out the material for my bag, I have two identical squares. Ideally, I will cut my squares so that the edges I sewed earlier will mark out the top of the bag. Before I cut my fabric, I mark out how large my bag will be. I add an extra quarter inch on every side to allow for seams. After the general shape is traced out on the fabric, I cut out my bag.

This is the point where I start sewing. First I separate the pieces and fold down the top so my bag will not have a raw edge at the opening. Once this fold is sewn in place, I line the pieces back up, nice sides together. I only want to sew the sides and bottom together, so I put a few pins along those three sides, far enough in that they won't catch on the foot of my sewing machine.

After that, it's just a single line of stitches along the sides and bottom. Then I remove the pins and turn the bag right-side out. Voila, a custom spell bag! Although the pattern is simple enough, my first few spell bags were pretty rough. It took some practice for me to get down how to properly fold the top edges and how to get the corners neatly untucked when the bag was turned right-side out. When I cast my spell, I fill the bag with whatever ingredients the spell calls for, then tie it shut with a length of ribbon, string, or cord.

This same bag pattern can be used to make storage bags for your divination or magical tools as well. You can even make a specialty bag for your grimoire, if you feel so inclined. And as you become more comfortable with the process, you might even find yourself sewing altar cloths, ritual clothes, and all manner of other magical supplies.

Mirror Boxes

Unlike spell bags, which are popular with witches in media, mirror boxes are something you might not have heard of before starting on your journey into the world of magic. Despite their lack of media presence, however, they are incredibly helpful. And, once you know how to make them, they are almost infinitely customizable so you can make the perfect box to suit your needs.

Mirror boxes are used in protective spells. A doll or trinket is placed inside that represents the person in need of protection. The mirrored exterior of the box is a physical representation of magical or psychic barriers that have been raised around this person. When negative energy is directed at the person, whether from another person or from a spiritual entity, the mirrors reflect the energy back to its source. These spells can also be adjusted to give the person "inside" the box a sense of serenity be reflecting back any energy that seeks to distract them.

But protective spells are not all these boxes are good for. If the mirrored exterior is jagged, any energy sent back its source will take on a "sharp" edge and inflict an amount of discomfort specified when the box is created. Some witches are uncomfortable with magic that has an edge to it. But if you are comfortable with such magic, mirror boxes are an excellent way to limit the effect to such spells to those who seek to inflict harm first.

Mirror boxes can also be used to encourage self-reflection. As with any spell, this should not be used on someone without their consent. But when you have the person's consent, it is very easy to create a mirror box where the mirrors are on the inside rather than the outside. Then the item symbolizing the spell's target is put inside, encouraging self-reflection. When you use mirror boxes in this way, you can leave the exterior blank or paint it with messages that further support the self-reflection.

To construct a mirror box you first need to get the box. The exact size will depend on the item you are using to represent the target of the spell. For the most part, I use the paperboard boxes from craft stores. Occasionally I will use a cardboard box from my kitchen, if it suits the size I need. Once you have your box, you need to find your reflective material. Most craft stores sell mirrored tiles. But you can also use broken pieces of CDs and glue them down like mosaic tiles. Or, if you want to create the more aggressive form of the box, glue them with a point sticking outward. Other popular materials include tin foil or sheets or reflective plastic that you can get at craft stores or thrift stores.

You can use any adhesive that works for the reflective material you chose. And the object that symbolizes the spell's target will vary from person to person. I have personally used necklace charms from the craft store, miniature people intended for miniature ceramic villages, and paper dolls that resembled my friends.

If you are casting the spell for a long period of time, you may also want to include a soft cushion on the bottom of the box. This is not strictly necessary, but it will represent the spell's target residing in comfort while the spell is in effect. And if you are seeking to do good with your spell, that can only be a good thing.

Witch Jars

The final project I want to walk you through are witch jars. There are two main kinds of witch jars and I intend to teach you how to make both versions. All witch jars are made the same way, they simply vary in their contents and intended effects. To make one, you just need to get a jar and fill it with ingredients that suit the needs of your spell.

Most witch jars can be made in old jam jars. And, truth be told, recycling a previously used jar is exactly the sort of things our foremothers would have done. If you want to use a new jar, however, Mason jars are an excellent option that are durable, easy to find, and come in a wide range of sizes.

When choosing the size of your jar, there are a few things you have to consider. The first, and most important, is that you are probably going to be burying your witch jar. Reusing an old gallon-sized jar is a good way to reduce waste but if you are not comfortable digging a hole that big for it, you might want to spring for a smaller jar from the thrift store or ask a friend if you can have their jam jar when they are done with it.

You also have to bear in mind the things you are putting into your jar. Most witch jar ingredients are very small. It will be hard to fill a very large jar. On the other hand, if you want to do a custom witch jar once you are more comfortable with the process, you might find yourself in need of a much larger jar. It is all about your specific spell and its needs.

Once you have your jar, it is time to add the fillings. What you put in your jar, however, depends on the goal you want to achieve. Most witch jars are used either as house blessings or house protections. And though these two goals are very similar, the jars contain very different items. Blessing jars tend to focus on things that people want to bring into their homes or the homes of loves one. Home protection jars, on the other hand, are filled with items that will drive away anyone or anything that intends harm toward those who live inside the home.

Common items in a house blessing jar include:

- Images of bread or vegetables so that those inside the home will never know hunger

- Green or gold stones to represent money or wealth, so that the home will never feel the pinch of an empty wallet or financial need

- Soft fabric so that the residents will always have warm clothes and a warm place to sleep

- A secure lock so that the home's security will never be breached by those who do not have a key

- Cotton balls, poly filling, or feathers so that the lives of the home's inhabitants will be soft and comfortable.

- A small handwritten poem professing friendship, love, or appreciation for those in the house to support and cement your friendship with them, even if they are your own housemates or if the jar is for your own home.

Items in home protection jars, on the other hand, are usually much more aggressive:

- Nails, screws, tacks, broken glass, or push pins to cause discomfort or pain to any who would harm those living in the home

- Vinegar, lemon juice, or other acidic fluids that will aggravate wounds caused by the sharp objects

- A few handwritten lines declaring the intention of the jar and limiting its scope to those who would do willful harm

For some magic users, this jar edges a little too close to many forms of curses. And though not all witches avoid magical acts like curses or hexes, enough do that it is important for a distinction to be drawn. Curses and hexes are magic that take an offensive position. They will seek out the target the spell before the target can cause another act of direct harm. Witch jars, on the other hand, will only react when a harmful action is taken or planned and the person sets foot within the property the jar protects. It is a defensive spell, albeit a very aggressive one.

Whichever jar you choose to make, you can assemble it with or without protective barriers in place. You then want to charge it with your intention and, if you want to seal the intention more aggressively, set the jar under the full moon for a night. When it is ready, bury the jar at least a foot underground beside the house's front door. You can also bury it buy the front gate of there is a gate between the edge of the property and the home.

When the family moves or you feel the jar's effect is wearing off, you can dig up the jar and empty the contents. If you chose to make a protection jar, it may be best to shatter the jar into a trash receptacle where nobody will get hurt, or to dump it far from the home and recycle all the pieces. This will help prevent any negative energy caught within the jar from latching onto you or the people the jar was protecting.

As you become more comfortable with witch jars, you may find yourself creating new ones. Although blessing and protection jars are the most common, the creation process can be used for many purposes. You might want to try a dream collection jar, a creativity encouragement jar, or a focus jar to aid with meditation. All of these are made by finding objects that you connect to the cause in mind and infusing the jar with your intention. Witch jars are wonderfully variable things, just as many DIY magical supplies are.

Chapter 3: Tools by Spell Type

Generally speaking, magical tools are wildly versatile. They can be used to represent intangible concepts or deities, to direct our energy, and to perform somewhat mundane tasks like cutting herbs or producing ash. In some spells, however, tools have very specific uses. And these uses vary from spell to spell.

There are also tools that appear most often with certain types of spells. These tools are usually limited to stones or herbs, but they can also be certain types of ritual clothing or items as well as items that only fit the theme of a certain spell. In this chapter, I will go over the way certain tools perform special functions depending on the spell you cast, as well as touch on a few tools that only appear for certain types of spells.

Love Spells

Love spells are rather controversial in the magical community. If done incorrectly, they are considered a sort of magical Roofie. They take away someone's free will and cause them to act in a way they do not want to act. Even when done right – when the spell only calls for a certain kind of energy to enter your life in a romantic capacity – some magic users still find them distasteful. Before learning how certain tools are used in love spells, you should consider your stance on the spells themselves. From there, you can decide if this section is for you.

For those who approve of love spells, I feel I must clarify that I do not condone love spells cast on specific people. All of the tools in this section for intended for spells that do not target a person. Instead, these tools should be used to call a certain kind of energy into your life so that it can connect with you on a romantic or sexual level. At no point should you use this information to get a specific person to see you in a romantic or sexual fashion.

With that rule firmly in place, we can move on to the tools themselves. As I said at the beginning of the chapter, tools serve many purposes. When you are casting a love spell, the tools take on some very unique purposes. If your magic is influenced by Wiccan practices, you can use your wand or ceremonial knife to represent a male partner while your chalice can represent a female partner. Using any combination of these two items can symbolize you and your partner joining together in a relationship. And, if you are polyamorous, you can use more than two.

Certain stones and flowers also make appearances in love spells, though they are rarely seen in other magical workings. Rose quartz is a very popular stone in love spells, as its pink hue speaks the current modern association between the color pink and romantic love. And quartz itself is an incredibly versatile and useful stone that takes energy very well while being easy to find.

Roses are also very common in love spells. Many spell sachets geared toward finding love will combine rose petals and rose quartz with sweet-smelling herbs and a few other trinkets. These are then placed under the hopeful lover's bed or carried in their pocket until they find the love they are looking for. As with the color pink, red roses are seen as a sign of romantic love in many countries, which is why they are used in spells like these.

Indeed, most spell bags for love spells are red or pink. The color also makes an appearance as the thread color in spell braids or the thread that bundles together herbs that may be hung around a hopeful lover's door. Some people may also incorporate lace or silk, as these are very tactile fabrics often found in lingerie and other clothing designed with romance in mind.

Moon Spells

Any spell that relies on the timing and energy of the moon is a moon spell. Given that the spells rely so heavily on our nearest celestial neighbor, it makes sense that most of the tools and items used in these spells would either display or represent the moon. That is to say, witches who predominantly practice moon magic will usually have ritual knives, chalices, and other tools that all bear the image of the moon. They may even go so far as to get a tattoo of the moon, so as to tie themselves more closely to it.

As with love spells, there are certain stones that appear more often in moon spells than they do anywhere else. Moonstone – also known as hecatolite – and opals are found in many moon spells. Both of them are usually predominantly white, as the moon appears in the sky, but bear a rainbow-like sheen when looked at from certain angles. This sheen is said to represent the energy of the moon.

Many witches, particularly those influenced by Wicca, see the moon as a source of female energy. And, for this reason, statues of goddesses are also more common in moon spells. It should be noted, however, than in some cultures the moon explicitly represents a male deity. So the connection of the moon to female energy is not set in stone. As was true with correspondence charts, you should always go with what feels right to you when it comes to the moon's energy.

Common colors in moon spells include very, very light blues – which also relate to the color of the moon or its aura – and very dark blue. Very dark blues are more representative of the night sky, but they are an excellent backdrop for the brilliant stones mentioned above.

Many moon spells also focus on the use of moon water. I briefly touched on moon water in the section on charging and cleansing your tools, but I want to cover it a little more fully here. Moon water is any water that has been charged with the energy of the moon. This is usually done by putting the water in a clear glass container and then leaving this container in direct moonlight for a given length of time. The exact length of time varies based on the witch as well as the purpose of the moon water. Moon water can charge in moonlight for as little one night or as long as one entire lunar cycle, which is nearly a full month.

Some moon water is charged during very specific phases of the moon. Full Moon Water is usually used for protective spells, fertility spells, and spells to ease menstrual pain. Water from the New Moon is used for banishing spells, cleansing spells, and more aggressive protection spells than full moon water can produce. Witches who rely on moon magic will often charge a great deal of moon water all at once and then save it for use throughout the rest of the lunar cycle.

It is important to note that any water left out under the moon will not become moon water. For water to become Moon Water, it must be placed in a vessel with intention. That intention must then carry through when the vessel is placed in moonlight. Without this intention to mark the jar of water as important, the energy of the moon will simply pass it by.

This intention is what makes most tools effective for magic working. Without the guidance of your energy, the energy of spell will not know where to go or why it should be following the direction of your tools. If a spell is a car, then the energy you raise is the gas you put into it and your intention is the steering wheel. It is your best – and, really, your only – option when you want to steer the energy around you or the spell it is powering. This is just as true when charging Moon Water as it is with any other spell.

Nature Spells

For some witches, all spells are nature spells. Their energy is rooted in nature and the majority of their magical practice is rooted in a religion that honors the earth as a deity in and of itself. When you are this heavily immersed in nature, all of your tools bear nature energy and are for nature spells.

If nature is only *part* of your practice, however, there are a few things you can do to more closely align yourself with natural energies. This will be particularly helpful if you are trying to get your garden to grow better, learn something about the land on which your home is situated, or if you want to try and influence the weather in any way. Nature magic is also good for bringing out the nutrients in food and protecting your pets, as well as working larger spells with other witches to protect the wider natural world.

To more fully tap into natural energies, you should use tools made from natural materials. Yes, metal is technically a natural material. But it is harder to extract from the earth and takes a great deal more processing. Natural magic responds best to items made of natural clay or of wood. You can gather both of these straight from the earth without too much effort, depending on where you live of course. And, with a little practice, you can shape them into just about anything as well. This, of course, brings you right back to the benefits of DIY magical tools.

Choosing items made of wood or natural clay might not be enough, of course. If you choose a wand or cup made from a rare or frequently exploited wood, such as mahogany, you are not going to get a positive reaction from the natural energy you are trying to work with. You would have better luck using a stick from your backyard as a wand. Quite literally, actually, as it would have a stronger connection to you and could be gathered without harming the trees in any way.

You can just as easily connect the rest of your tools to the natural world as well. Stones and herbs are already closely connected to the natural world, of course. But if you get your stones from a quarry that is open to the public, you will have a much more intense connection to them. The same thing will happen if you have something of a green thumb and can grow your own herbs. They will grow in soil that is protected by your magic and can then be harvested with a dedicated harvesting knife (in some practices, these are referred to as bolines). All of this creates a connection between you and the herbs so that they are even more effective when used in your spells.

Kitchen witches – witches who infuse their food and drinks with magic – will find this particularly useful. Handling their herbs from seed or cutting all the way to the cooking pot allows them to connect with the plant's magic from the very beginning. So when they go to add the plants to their cooking, the magical addition is even stronger.

If you are able to grow your own herbs, make sure you charge all of the gardening tools you use. Everything from your gloves to your watering can to the hose you use, can be charged with the intention of infusing magic into the green growing things around you. You can also infuse fresh energy into the plants every time you settle in to tend them. This incorporates meditation as a sort of magical tool, which is something I cover in the final chapter of this book.

City Spells

You might not be familiar with the idea of city spells. But as more and more witches are bringing their practice into the modern world, spells focused on life in cities are becoming more common. These spells are usually designed to deal with traffic, rude people on public transport, or even to keep pests at bay in uniquely modern situations.

City spells also usually rely on the energy of a city. The thrum of all the vehicles, the hum of countless human voices, the heat that only rises above a large city. All of these things – and so much more – are part of what set the energy of city magic apart from other forms of magic. There are natural witches that practice within the label of modern witches, of course. And many of them practice in cities. But city magic usually refers to using the energy and materials found in a more manmade world.

This does not mean that you should run out and buy tools that are all brand new, however. Instead, it means trying to fit your practice as organically into your daily life as possible. This touches on another interesting argument in the magical community, however. Many witches feel that modern life is too plastic. And since plastic is causing so many problems for both humans and the animals we share the world with, it seems counterintuitive to use plastic in your magical practice, which is supposed to support a healthy life so that your magic remains healthy as well. You will have to wrestle with this issue yourself and see where your feelings lie.

One way to work city magic into your practice is by buying your tools from a thrift store. You will have to cleanse everything you buy before you use it for magic, of course. But there is something very satisfying about finding a gorgeous wine glass at the thrift store and taking it home to function as your chalice. Or in finding a beautiful ornamental knife and cleaning it up to serve as a ritual knife. It will never cut anything, not while it serves as your ritual knife. But it looks amazing as it directs your energy in your rituals.

You can also find ritual clothing, scrap material, and candles at the thrift store. If you go often enough, you can find everything you need for either magical or mundane purposes. And the truly amazing thing about this is that thrift stores are unique to city life. In smaller towns, there might be a single thrift store that is part of a larger chain. But, for the most part, people just have a yard sale or give to the church rummage sale. A whole superstore filled with previously loved items is something that only becomes possible when there are a lot of people all in one place.

Experienced witches can take this a step farther and may actually seek out items at the thrift store that have a unique energy to them. This then becomes an energy source for them or a focal point for their next spell. Novice witches should never attempt this, of course. There is a very high risk of picking something up with a toxic energy that is masked by an attractive exterior.

But shopping at thrift stores is only one way to tap into the energy of a city. If you live in a city with a lot of local pride, particularly if it is a big city, you can find lots of items printed with the city's name or iconic images of local landmarks. These can be very effective magical tools if you personally have a lot of pride in the city where you live.

You can also tap into the energy of a city using tools very specific to a large cities. These include bus tickets to show that you have traveled the city's roads, which can help you tape into the energy that builds up on streets and thoroughfares when they are traveled regularly. You can also use subway maps as magical tools by tracing the lines of the most populous routes to tap into the energy they generate.

If you do not live in a big city, you can do much the same thing with a layout of the electrical lines in your home. You can trace your finger over the blueprint lines and tap into the energy that runs through your walls. Over time, if you find that you are tracing specific sections repeatedly, you can turn this into a sigil that allows you quicker access to the energy of your home.

Adapting Tools for Your Spell

The tools and their uses outlined in this chapter are only a small sample of the way tools change depending on the spell you want to cast. But there are many, many more kinds of spells out there. And there is a good chance that you will come across spells where you want to use the tool you already have, but you want to have them align more fully with the energy of the spell you want to cast.

There are, thankfully, many ways that you can adapt your current tools to fit the energy source you want to use or the spell you are casting. Some tools, like candles, can be easily replaced. Because of this, you can etch shapes and words into them to merge them more fully with the intention of your spell. You can also fill the candle holder with objects that suit the spell. Seashells for a spell powered by the ocean is an excellent example. You just have to be sure that you don't mind getting wax on whatever is placed in the candle holder.

Other items, like your wand, can be wrapped in wire or thread that has been threaded with beads that match the intention of your spell. The colors would work best if they were taken from your own personalized correspondence chart. But some general suggestions are green and gold beads for money spells, yellow for spells to call in happiness, and black or grey beads for spells that encourage self-reflection.

Changing the color of your tools – even if it's just by wrapping them in different colors of ribbon – is a good way to adapt your tools to fit your spell. You can also turn everyday objects from around your home into magical tools by cleansing and then charging them. This allows you to substitute different items into your practice as needed without buying a whole new set of tools each time you try a new type of spell.

And, of course, you may find that you feel most comfortable using the same general tools for every spell. There is absolutely nothing wrong with this. If you do this, however, I do suggest you try adapting your tools to the spell at hand and see if that increases the efficacy of your magical workings.

Chapter 4: Divination as a Tool

Divination is a more accurate term for the practice that many people refer to as "fortune telling" or "seeing the future". True divination can tell you more than what kind of luck you have hanging around. It cannot, unfortunately, tell you the future. This is largely because the future is not set in stone. If it were, there would be no free will. But it is also because divination's energy is rooted in the things that have already happened and the things that are happening right this moment. Reaching into the future is an entirely different kind of energy than divination uses.

Many new magic users are disappointed when they find all of this out. But they should not be. Knowing the future would simply make life a little more boring. Being able to suss out hidden information – both past and present – is much more interesting. And the best part is that there are so many divination tools out there that everyone can find a method that works for them.

In this chapter I will cover the most common divination methods as well as a few modern practices that are quickly gaining popularity. You might notice that, despite my discussion of popular scrying methods, rune stones are not listed in this chapter. This is for two reasons. One is that runes are a rather touchy subject in the divination community. They originally started as an alphabet and many witches feel that using them for divination is a bit of a stretch. Though I touch on some controversies in this book, I am more interested in delivering as much information as I can, rather than working through both sides of the argument. I also opted to leave out runes because – both as divination tools and as alphabets – runes are wildly detailed. There are several runic alphabets and each one affects how they are used in divination. Runes, therefore, will simply have to wait for another time.

The divination practices in this chapter include oracle and tarot cards – the difference between which I will cover shortly -, several methods of scrying, pendulums, dreams, and omens. I will also be covering a few popular divination practices among modern witches and touching on how you can use modern devices to engage in divination.

Oracle and Tarot Cards

The most common – and commonly depicted – forms of divination are the cards. Popular media usually relies on tarot cards, though they mangle the meanings in the process. But there are many other kinds of divination cards that you can use. For the most part, these non-tarot divination cards fall under the umbrella term of "oracle cards".

There are several key differences between tarot cards and oracle cards. And it is important to know these differences before you try divining anything with a deck of cards. If you do not understand the differences before you get started, you might find that one kind of cards does not work well for you and mistakenly assume no cards will work.

Tarot is the divination system with major and minor arcana. These are the cards that typically appear in movies and on television shows "The five of wands" and "The Hanged Man" are both cards from the Rider-Waite style of tarot. One comes from the minor arcana and one from the major.

If you think "four of wands" sounds like something you'd see in a deck of playing cards with a magical theme, you are not far off from the origin of this divination tool. In part, tarot started as a storytelling game in Renaissance Italy. Friends would get together and draw cards, then make up stories and poems based on the meaning of the cards. This was sometimes played with the usual four-suit deck that we are used to today. At other times that cards would be more specialized.

When these two decks merged, they more or less produced the Rider-Waite tarot deck, so named for the men who formalized it as a divination tool. The original illustrations, which can easily be found with an internet search, were illustrated by Pamela Colman Smith. Because of Smith's vital involvement, this deck is also referred to as the Rider-Waite-Smith or the Waite-Smith deck as well.

As this deck grew in popularity, other decks emerged that used the same symbolic expectations but changed the illustrations and how the cards were used. These are still tarot decks, but they do not use the exact illustrations and descriptions of the Rider-Waite-Smith deck and are therefore referred to by other names. Decks that based their designs on the Rider-Waite-Smith deck usually make small changes – such as giving the deck a novel theme – and then distance themselves more fully by changing the illustrations and perhaps the suits of the minor arcana.

Another key difference between Rider-Waite-Smith tarot cards and other tarot cards is how upside-down cards are perceived. When a witch performs a reading with the Rider-Waite-Smith deck, an upside-down card is called in inverted card. And, when these appear, they mean the opposite of what the card usually means. If a card usually means abundance, it now means drought or a lack of something. And if a hard like the Hanged Man comes up, where it signifies the reading's subject not seeing things clearly, it means they are seeing clearly despite what others might think.

This difference is minor but vital. It can completely change the outcome of a reading. But compared the differences between tarot cards and oracle cards, this difference is absolutely minor. Unlike tarot cards, oracle cards have no major and minor arcana. The cards may be numbered as they are in tarot decks, but that is more so that newcomers can easily look up card meanings in the books that usually come with divination decks.

It might seem silly to include an entire book with a divination deck. But if you have never cracked open the book that comes with a divination deck, I strongly advise you to give it a try, even if you don't think cards will work as a divination form for you. These books are backed with amazing information that can benefit your practice even if you are not one for divination at all.

For the most part, these books contain layouts you can use with your cards. But, more than that, they contain detailed descriptions of the cards. The descriptions almost always explain why the artist and deck creator chose the symbols that they did, sometimes with so much detail that they explain the color choice as well. If you are trying to work on a correspondence chart, finding an oracle card that resonates with you and then reading the reasoning behind its design is a great way to see what that image meant to someone else. From there, you can see what you agree with and meditate on where you differ from the card's creator.

Oracle cards are much more open than tarot cards as well. They do not have major or minor arcana, as I already said. But they also tend to use very organic imagery. A frog in a card, for example, will often represent something very easily associated with a frog, like patience or moving between two seemingly different worlds. Oracle decks may also be smaller, which is helpful for people who might not feel that they need a full 78-card tarot deck or who would struggle to shuffle that many at once. Of course, this also means that there are fewer cards which may lead to more general readings. But, for beginners, this might be a good thing.

And, no matter which form of divination card you choose, there is always a third option when you want to perform a reading. Once you are comfortable with the cards and have spent enough time with them to know their names from just a glance at the image, you may find that your perception of them begins to change. You might know the card creator's reasoning for their design as well as you know your own bedroom furniture. But after a while, you may find that you stop agreeing with the creator's view of the cards as your own begins to form.

This happens to a great many card readers. It usually takes a few years of using the same cards. But over time, you and your cards create a bond. They are not just pieces of paper but a channel through which you make contact with your higher power or the spirits that guide your readings. And as you get comfortable with this connection, you will feel your own energy soaking into the cards, marking them as part of you and your practice.

And when this happens, you will begin to understand the cards on a new level. Maybe one card in your deck bears the image of bread and wine, which the creator of the deck said was meant to symbolize community. But after you have used the deck for a great deal of time, you come to find that – in your readings at least – it actually means getting back to basics or enjoying the finer things in life, or something else entirely. This does not mean that the creator of the deck was wrong. Rather, it means that you and your deck are communicating with one another. And that is a kind of magic that is so intimate and so breathtaking that it can change how you approach the rest of your magic.

If you feel that cards might be your ideal divination tool, do not just run out and buy the first deck that you see at the bookstore. And, for the most part, bookstores always carry divination cards. Instead, spend some time browsing online metaphysical shops. If you find a deck of cards you like, see if you can find the creator's website and browse the other decks they may have. There is a myth out there that someone has to buy your first deck of cards for you. But that is all it is. A myth.

Many witches focus on the art when they buy a deck of divination cards. This is because you will spend most of your time staring at the art on the cards when you work with them. Some witches go so far as to have a favorite artist whose decks they buy every time a new one comes out. Others just buy whatever decks strike their fancy and move between them as their tastes change. And then there are witches who buy one deck of cards and that is their only deck. They use it faithfully for the entirety of their magical life. If you choose to read cards, you will find yourself in one of these camps.

Even if you are the kind of witch who only ever uses a single deck, however, there is still one final warning that you must know. And it is this: card reading witches love to collect divination decks. I personally have over a dozen, although I only read with one or two. There is just something comforting about a deck of divination cards. And so many of them are oh so pretty. You have been warned!

Scrying in Water, Flame, and Smoke

Divination cards may be the popular form of divination in modern media. But scrying is quite likely the oldest form of divination, second only to reading omens and portents in the world around us. Portents and omens will be discussed later in this chapter. For now, however, we are going to talk about scrying.

Scrying, in general, is the act of looking into an organically moving thing and letting your mind follow the patterns there until they reveal the information you seek. This is most often done in water, flame, and smoke. You can also scry in a mirror whose back has been painted black, using the light that reflects off the mirror's surface. But this is a more specialized form of scrying and, as a beginner, it would be easier to stick with the three forms we will discuss in this section.

All three basic variations on scrying work the same way. You sit in a comfortable place – because scrying can take a while – and stare into the medium you have chosen. After a time your eyes will shift out of focus and this is a good thing. Let your gaze follow whatever patterns they will as you focus your mind on the topic you want to learn about. The patterns your mind picks up on will bear the messages you need.

Scrying works best if you have already practiced your focus and mindfulness. Both grounding and centering are excellent ways to practice this talent and I cover both extensively in my book *The Beginner Witch*. I will also cover them in the last chapter of this book. And though I give a guided practice for each exercise, the descriptions are focus more on how to use them as tools rather than as basic overviews.

Once you have confidence in your ability to ground and center, however, you will find that scrying comes much more naturally.

Rather than chasing specific thoughts or chiding yourself for losing focus, you can easily bring your thoughts back to where they need to be while tracking the patterns in your scrying focus.

And you may find, as you start scrying, that it is already something you have done without realizing it. Many people have simply sat and stared into a lake or watched the flames dance while they let their minds wander. And, as they do, revelations or ideas suddenly occur to them. This, in part, is what scrying does. As a witch, you simply have more control over how and when you scry.

This intuitive approach to scrying is a good indication that it will be the ideal form of divination for you. And it also serves to highlight why scrying has been part of human culture for so long. Society as we know it is said to have begun when we had regular access to water and the ability to control fire. So it makes sense that when we had the time and ability to sit down and ponder the water, fire, and smoke around us that we were able to connect with the messages waiting inside.

Some modern witches have found that they can scry in the static on a television screen or the white noise over a set of headphones. Other witches – largely due to horror movie tropes – find this prospect terrifying and prefer to stick to the older methods. If you find that scrying works for you, I encourage you to try all of these methods. Just be sure you engage your sense of discernment and, just maybe, try scrying with a barrier or two in place.

With the more traditional methods, a barrier is still a good idea. But raising a protective barrier around certain scrying source might be tricky if you are trying to do it on your own. Bonfires, for instance, are fantastic places to scry. They contain a great deal of fire, energy, and smoke. But they are also very large and, as such, your protective wards would have to cover a very large amount of ground. If you are attending a bonfire hosted by other witches, however, there is a good chance that the entire property has been warded. In these cases, you can scry safely without erecting your own wards.

Water, too, can be difficult to scry in if you are trying to raise your own wards. While scrying in lakes, rivers, and oceans is a fantastic and deeply moving experience, water does not take well to being divided by protective wards. It will simply wash away any barrier to try to put down on a body of water that large. Instead, you might find it easier to use a form of psychic armor, as I describe in *The Beginner Witch* so that you can safely scry in large bodies of water.

Barring this, your next best choice is to ask the body of water if you can collect enough for a scrying bowl. When you receive an affirmative flow of energy, collect enough water to fill anything from a cereal bowl to a mixing bowl. You then take this home and use it to scry within the safety of your own wards. When the water runs out – either through evaporation or through gradual loss as you pour it between the bowl and the container you collected it in – you can return to the source and ask for more.

If you want to scry with fire or smoke and bonfires are not a convenient means, you can always use a candle or incense. Most witches keep at least one of these on their altars at all times. So scrying with smoke or flame from this source is as easy as raising your wards around your altar, settling into a comfortable position, and lighting the candle or settling the incense into a smolder.

When scrying with flame it is best to have the lights down low so that you can focus on the flame. With smoke, however, you want the lights at roughly half their normal brightness. This will let you see the smoke but will not be so bright that you cannot make out the specific shape of it. Water, on the other hand, can be read at just about any light level. You will not be able to see much in a pitch black room. But the difference in light level can create new depths to the water when you scry, giving you even more information.

Over time, you may find that scrying with one medium no longer works. This is a completely normal part of evolving on your magical path. You may change the medium you scry with or how you find the patterns when you scry. You might even find that your preferred form of divination completely changes. As you change as a person, you will change as a witch and this is just something to be expected.

Pendulums

Next to divination cards, pendulums are probably the commonly depicted forms of divination in modern media. And, just as with divination cards, media gets it close but embellishes a few things. Pendulums are amazing divination tools but they will not immediately point to the location of something you have lost. On the other hand, most media portrays pendulums as capable of strictly giving yes or no answers. And this is also not true.

The truth of pendulums lies somewhere in the middle. This is somewhat fitting as they are a moderately difficult divination medium to use. They are not quite as intuitive as scrying. But they do not require as much studying as divination cards. In order to use a pendulum, you need to have a fairly strong grasp on both your magical abilities and your thoughts. You must be able to control both, at least to a moderate degree.

Without this level of control, your pendulum is not going to find any answers. Instead, it will either spin in circles, dance wildly, or not move at all. With a little control, however, you can communicate with your pendulum and find a language that will help you find the answers you need. Controlling your magic allows you to open up this line of communication. Having control of your thoughts, on the other hand will help you maintain control over the direction of your questions.

In addition to having a proper level of control, you also need to find the best pendulum for your practice. You can make a pendulum out of nearly anything, so long as the weight of the pendant is evenly distributed and you have it properly attached to a long string, chain, or cord. If you are not up to making your own, however, metaphysical shops usually offer a wide variety of pendulums. They come in all shapes and sizes. And, more importantly, they come in a wide range of materials.

The three most common materials are metal, stone, and wood. Metal pendulums are usually etched or cast with mythical creatures or magical symbols. Some are even hollow so that they can be filled with herbs or, if your handwriting is small enough, a minute scroll that can contain anything from a spell to a single word that focuses the intention of your pendulum work.

Stone or crystal pendants are almost always a single piece, inset with a small metal hoop through which it is threaded onto a length of string or a thin chain. Pendulums made of stones and crystals tend to end in sharper points, due to the nature of the material's structure. They are particularly useful if you are using your pendulum to narrow your focus to a particular image or a single word in a book. I will explain this use in a little more detail further on in the section. It is quite useful, but not as dramatic as television would have you believe.

The final common variants on pendulums are those made of wood. These are usually – but not always – made as a single piece. A few rare wooden pendulums are hollow with a top that screws in, much like the metal ones. They too can be filled with herbs or small flakes of stone to further the focus of your divination work. It should be noted that neither the wooden nor the metal variant of hollow pendulums should be filled with liquid. Not only will this warp a wooden pendulum and potentially rust one made of metal, but the liquid will move in ways that can completely disrupt a divination practice.

Once you have chosen the best material for your pendulum and found one that feels right for your practice, it is time to cleanse your pendulum. This will remove any unwanted energy from other people who handled it at the shop or at the warehouse from which it was shipped. After cleansing your pendulum, you will want to charge it with your energy while you are connected with whatever higher power or spirits you choose to work with. This connection is what makes the pendulum effective at turning up new information or uncovering that which is hidden, because these spirits and energies can see things we cannot.

As with all divination tools, it is best to start off with easy questions. Witches will typically start with questions they already know the answers to, particularly with pendulums. This is to get a feel for how the tool answers in the affirmative or the negative. When it comes to pendulums, there are a few ways that the tools establish this basic communication style.

Some common combinations included swinging back and forth for "yes" or side to side for "no", or moving in a clockwise circle for "yes" and in a counter-clockwise for "no". You might find that your pendulum follows these patterns or inverts them. Or you might be one of the rare few whose pendulums develop their own signals, though this usually only happens with experienced witches.

Once you have established this baseline communication style with your pendant, it is a good idea to spend some time asking more yes and no questions. At the beginning of this section I mentioned that pendulums can do more than answer yes and no questions. And they can. But divination is like any other skill. You want to work up to the more difficult processes by practicing the simple ones until they are second nature.

A good way to practice easy pendulum work is to ask yes and no questions that you know the answer to, intermingled with questions you do not know the answers to. Or, at the very least, questions whose answers you are unsure of. As you master this technique, you will learn how to branch your questions so that one answer leads to another and then another.

When this process is easy, you can move on to the more difficult pendulum methods. These vary from witch to witch, as nearly all magical practices do. But there are a few popular methods that can yield a great deal of information for the witch who has properly connected with their pendulums.

The first of these is an answer mat. As the name implies, this is a sheet of paper or piece of fabric with answers, letters, symbols, and numbers written on it. In some ways, it closely resembles a Ouija board. Unlike the board, however, there is no single prescribed method for how the answers should be written on the paper or fabric.

You can find a dizzying number of pendulum answer boards online. But if you enjoyed this book's section on DIY magic tools, you might enjoy the challenge of making your own answer board. A simple version would consist of a piece of paper or cardboard with the answers written on it in a way that seems organic to you. More complex versions could include painted boards or materials with the answers hand-embroidered in place. Witches who practice privately can even hide their answer boards in plain sight by making them look like table cloths, ornate table tops, or decorations like wall hangings.

Using an answer mat is a little more complicated than getting a yes or no out of your pendulum. But if pendulums respond well to your energy, you will quickly find yourself adept at finding the answers you need. Divination always works best if you ground and center first. From there, you can close your eyes and ask your question. When your pendulum begins to move, you will feel it pulling you in a specific direction. Once it finds the answer it seeks, it will either stop moving entirely or circle slowly above the answer. The longer you use this method, the easier it will be and the more readily your pendulum will divulge its answers.

Earlier I mentioned that you can use pendulums with books and maps to find information or try and locate lost things. Many popular forms of media use this method and depict the pendulum snapping into place above the important words or locations. The reality is not quite so cut and dried. Using your pendulum with a map or book is a lot like using it with an answer mat. You must let your pendulum guide your hand pay close attention to where it stops.

Pendulum divination is quite possibly the easiest form of divination to use while on the go. You just have to make sure that you have the answer key, if you use one. And you must be sure that your pendulum is properly stored when you are traveling. If a pendulums point is damaged – or if it is stone and cracks – it may not answer you quite as clearly. And, in some cases, it will stop working entirely.

Modern Divination Practices

Most of the divination practices in use today came down to us through myths, legends, ancient texts, and a groups of people that kept the ancient practices alive. Some practices, however, are either entirely new concepts or have put a very modern spin on ancient practices. I cover these in great detail in my book *Modern Witchcraft for Beginners*. I will cover them again here, but if you want more information I strongly suggest picking up a copy so that you can explore these topics in more depth.

The most common of the thoroughly modern divination methods is shufflemancy. At the same time that this method became more popular, bibliomancy also saw a rise in popularity as well. This connection might have been intentional, as the methods can be used together. I will explain both and then walk you through how they can be combined in case these methods or the combination thereof speaks to you.

Shufflemancy is an incredibly modern concept. It uses principles that have appeared on and off in other divination method. But the way shufflemancy employs them is unique to this specific approach. To perform shufflemancy, a witch need only put a form of media on shuffle and focus their thoughts on the topic or question they want to explore.

When it was first popularized, shufflemancy was usually only performed with music. Over time, however, other forms of media became more common. The exact method varies depending on the type of media being used. But they all fall under the umbrella of shufflemancy so long as the witch's media library is put on shuffle so that the higher power or spirits she works with can influence the exact song, episode, or whatever else that comes up.

Using shufflemancy with music is easiest and this is probably why it was the first method that gained popularity. The more music a witch has, the more and specific her answers can be. Some witches restrict their divination to the titles of the songs, gleaning meaning from the phrasing and tone of the title. Others take things a step further by listening to the song and finding which lyrics stand out the most to them.

Music witches find this method particularly useful. If they understand the structure of music, they may find meaning in the actual flow of the music as well as the lyrics or title. And, as I said, the more music there is the better the answers will be. So witches with large digital music libraries or access to randomized streaming music may find that shufflemancy is the easiest way for them to dive deeply into any given topic.

If you feel that shufflemancy is your idea divination form, I suggest starting with single songs for single questions. This will allow you to take your time with the song and make sure that you are reading it correctly. Once this has become easy, you can move on to shuffling entire playlists and moving from one song to the next to answer extensive questions or dig deeply into hidden topics.

As the use of shufflemancy spread, new media forms came to be used. This was made easier with the advent of streaming media that provided a wide range of television shows and movies for witches who connect strongly with these media forms. Though it might seem odd to use popular media as a form of divination in itself – particularly given media's tendency to depict older divination forms incorrectly – it actually makes perfect sense. Popular media is modern humanity's way of processing the world around us. Or, in some cases, our way of coping with the world around us. They are modern myths. And this makes them ideal for divination.

Applying shufflemancy to songs is relatively straightforward, since most digital music services offer a shuffle feature. Using shufflemancy with television and movies, however, is a little more difficult, though it is certainly possible. If you want to give it a try and you have a digital streaming service, start by going into a menu of as many titles as possible. If your service breaks titles down by genres, you can close your eyes and use your remote to select a genre, seemingly at random. As with all divination, however, it is not random. It is guided by the spirits and higher powers you work with.

Once you are on a list of specific titles, close your eyes and repeat the process I described above for selecting a genre. If you select a movie, you will have to search your own sense of your reading to determine if you need to watch the whole thing. Sometimes, you will. At other times, however, you only need a specific scene. On these occasions, close your eyes once again and begin fast forwarding through the movie. Your spirits or higher power will urge you to stop when it is time. Likewise, they will give you a sense of when you have seen the portion you need to see.

Television shows are used in much the same way, but with one added step. Rather than starting at the first episode, repeat the seemingly random selection process going through first the seasons and then the episodes with the season. From there you can repeat the process of either watching the entire episode or fast forward through the sections that you do not need for your reading.

If you are using a physical collection of movies or television shows, you will use a similar process to select the specific media form. Rather than flipping through genres and seasons with your remote, however, you will close your eyes and follow the urges of your guiding forces until your finger rests on the spine of the case you need. From there you will repeat the fast forwarding step. If the case contains multiple discs, perform the guided motions you used to select the case in the first place.

This method might seem wholly modern. But, as I mentioned earlier, the basic principle of this divination practice has been used with much older forms of psychic reading. Divination cards are an excellent example of ways that this seemingly random method is much older than streaming media.

For centuries, card readers have required that their cards be shuffled by the person who wants the reading. It might be them or it might be someone else. In either case, shuffling the cards while the person focuses on their question served as a way to make sure the cards were attuned to the right person and the right questions. More often than you might think, cards would fall out of the deck during the shuffling process. These cards were set aside because, depending on the reader and the topic of the reading, they held important meanings.

Usually the cards that fell out of the deck were used to set the tone for the reading. If they were largely positive cards, everything laid out during the reading was seen in a more hopeful light. However, if the cards were meant to deliver warning or to urge caution, even positive cards in the reading were taken with a grain of salt. This is not quite the same thing as allowing your guiding powers to guide your music or television choices. But the seemingly random nature of the cards that fell from the deck – and the uncertain nature of when they would fall – make this practice a natural precursor to modern shufflemancy.

And, as I mentioned earlier, shufflemancy dovetails perfectly into another form of divination known as bibliomancy. This divination technique might be listed as a modern divination method, but that is largely because its current popularity is a fairly modern creation. Forms of bibliomancy have existed for as long as people have had relatively common access to books or other printed media. As books became more common – and their content more varied – bibliomancy became more popular.

The beauty of bibliomancy is that it can easily be adapted for any type of witchcraft. Although bibliomancy is most popular among "word witches" or "book witches" who focus their magic – and, by extension, their divination – through the written word, anyone can access this form of magic. All they need to do is find a book that resonates with their particular form of witchcraft.

Book witches tend to prefer fiction books or books of old fairy tales and myths, because they relate not only to the words in the book but also with the themes and structures of the stories. These witches are often people who enjoy deconstructing books on a mundane level. So when they select a book and then a passage from that book seemingly at random, it is relatively easy for them to dig out the meaning they are supposed to find.

But you do not need to have a love of reading to use bibliomancy. You could in fact only own one book, the one you use for divination, and it can still be an effective magical tool for you. So long as you can relate to and understand the contents of the book and how they relate to your practice, it is a good tool for your practice.

To perform bibliomancy readings, select the book you want to use. If you have several to choose from, you can close your eyes and let your higher power or spiritual connections guide your finger to the right book. From there, you flip through the book, stop when you feel the urge to, and then run your finger along the page. If you have chosen a book with images, you may find that your finger stops on the images rather than on text. This still counts as bibliomancy, though most forms of bibliomancy involve reading and interpreting a passage of the book in your hands.

This method can work with nearly any printed media from magazines to leaflets to religious texts. So long as you can interpret what you are looking at, you can use it for bibliomancy.

These are only the most common forms of modern divination. There are others that employ search engine results, the motion of traffic, and other such things to divine meaning in the every day flow of modern life. These methods are more convoluted, however. So beginning witches are encouraged to start with the options outlined in this chapter and then move on when they feel that they understand these methods well enough.

It should also be noted that both shufflemancy and bibliomancy differ in some very key ways from the other forms of divination mentioned thus far in this book. The most obvious of these is that you do not have to charge or cleanse the items you use in these forms of divination. It would be very difficult to cleanse a media streaming service, for example. And while you can always cleanse and charge a book that is dedicated to magical purposes, this is harder to do if the book is borrowed from someone else or used for more mundane purposes.

You also do not need to cast protective wards around your computer, television, or phone before you perform these forms of divination. As is the case with water, the energy used to transmit your media will cut right through your barriers. It is better to use a personalized shield or form of psychic armor when performing these forms of divination. You can ward the area around you if you are using physical forms of media, of course. But if you are streaming something, you should stick with personal protection so as to leave nothing to chance.

These methods can also be combined with the other forms of divination that I have already mentioned. If you use a pendulum, you might find that combining your pendulum with the book set aside for bibliomancy yields interesting results. Likewise, using the book from a pack of divination cards as a bibliomancy book might lead to interesting places that neither method would reveal on their own.

Dreams

Dream interpretation, along with the portents and omens I will cover in the final section of this chapter – are two forms of divination that many people practice whether or not they consider themselves magic users. Like scrying, it is almost human intuition to look at the images that play across our minds when we sleep, then try to derive some sort of meaning from them.

There are many, many books on the market that cover dream interpretation in-depth. And, as with correspondence charts, these pre-made options are great for beginners. But, as you get more comfortable with interpreting your dreams, you may find that you do not agree with the definitions in your dream interpretation book.

When this happens, you have a few options. The first option is to go through and edit the book so that the various entries reflect your own experience. Over time, the book your purchased will come to reflect the way you interpret your own dreams. Unfortunately, this will also become rather crowded and, potentially, hard to read. You might even find your own symbol interpretation changing so you have to rewrite the meaning of various symbols more than once.

For a cleaner record of the way you interpret your dreams, you can create a dream interpretation section in your grimoire. This not only links your dreams and their interpretation more fully to your magical practice, but gives you more control over the layout and organization of the interpretations. Rather that crossing out old definitions and writing in new ones, you can recreate the entire entry. Or, if dream interpretation comes to be a large part of your magical practice, each symbol can have their own page. When a definition changes you can simply make a new page.

Your third option is a little more involved. And unless dream interpretation becomes key to your practice, it may be more effort than necessary. But witches who deal largely in dreams tend to keep dream journals. And a sort of interpretation key is usually included at the beginning of every dream journal so that the witch in question does not have to pull out a specific interpretation book each time they have a dream.

Of course, over time, any witch who regularly interprets her dreams will memorize the meanings of various symbols. But we all know that our minds are not at their best when they first wake up. It is much easier to interpret your dreams when you have something in front of you that can help you make connections.

Keeping track of your dreams and their meanings is a very handy magical tool. But, for the most part, this leaves the magic user at the whim of random dreams. If you want to use the dream as a regular divination tool, you will have to learn how to encourage your mind to dream. Although this book is focused more on magical tools than on spells, I would be remiss if I did not include a few simple ways for you to dream more regularly.

One of the easiest ways to encourage dreams is to find a stone or create a lavender sachet that you hold onto as you fall asleep. The feeling of the stone in your hand or the scent of lavender in your nose as you fall asleep will keep your mind on dreams as you drift off. Every time you smell lavender as you sleep or feel the rock in your hand, it will bring your mind back to the idea of dreams.

You have to be sure you are not allergic to lavender, of course. And if a stone is particularly sharp or prone to cracking or chipping, you will want to choose an alternative so that you do not cut yourself in your sleep. You might also find that your skin reacts oddly to some stones. Just as with lavender, you should be sure you are not allergic to your chosen stone before using it for a sleep spell.

Another method to encourage dreams is to essentially meditate on the idea of dreams before you go to sleep. Then, as you drift off, try to keep your mind on the thought of dreaming. Unfortunately, there are a few catches to this method. The first is that directing your thoughts as you drift off to sleep is very hard. This act can also serve to wake some people up, countering the whole purpose of laying down in the first place.

In addition to those drawbacks, this method may also open the door to lucid dreaming. And while lucid dreaming is a very important and useful branch of magic, that falls more under the exploration of the spiritual world that is done under the umbrella of divination. If you begin to lucid dream without any ideas as to how you can stop, you might cut yourself off from the ability to interpret your dreams entirely. Unfortunately, lucid dreaming is a very in-depth topic that, while fascinating, is too intensive to dive into this book.

Portents and Omens

The final section of this chapter is dedicated to a divination form that is almost as old as scrying. And, to a degree, better documented than any other form of divination. I am, of course, referring to interpreting portents and omens. As with lucid dreaming in the last chapter, it is hard to cover this in any real depth within a book that focuses on several different things. But it is an important tool for witches around the world and, as such, is something that I at least wanted to touch on.

There are portents and omens all around us, once we learn to look for them. Their meanings will vary depending on your cultural identity, religious views, and personal experience. But the way that you notice and then act on them is the same no matter what the symbols mean. The most important thing when it comes to portents and omens is to engage your discernment before acting on any that you see. If you're not completely certain of an omen's meaning, you may even want to apply one of the divination practices listed earlier in this chapter.

Once you have determined the meaning of an omen or portent, you have a few options. The first is that you can ignore it, more or less. You will be aware of it, of course. But you can just refuse to take action. If it is something negative, you can engage your personal wards and strengthen the wards around your home and loved ones. And if it is something gravely dangerous or something that may happen on a large scale, you can contact other witches to try and organize a large magical working to try and head off the situation.

Chapter 5: Meditation and Visualization as a Tool

The final group of tools that we are going to cover are those of meditation and visualization. I will cover both grounding and centering, which are core practices in most witchcraft paths. After giving a brief explanation of each, I will provide a guided practice for each. From there we will move into the way meditation and visualization can affect your spellwork. Finally, I will touch on Shadow work, including what it is and how it can impact your religious and magical practices in addition to your mundane life.

Grounding

You have probably heard of meditation. In fact, you might have participated in a meditation practice in a retreat of some kind or a yoga class. But even if you have meditated before, there is a chance you might not have been instructed in the art of grounding yourself. And it is even less likely that you have instructed on how grounding your energy affects your magical practice. Although the process is similar to standard meditation, the focus is a little bit different.

When you ground for magical purposes, your focus is not so much on emptying your mind as on taking stock of your energy levels and their content. Later on, in the centering section, you will learn how to control where your energy goes. But before you can take that step, you have to learn how to read your energy. And grounding is the best way to do this.

Typically, a witch grounds for one of two reasons. The first reason is to anchor herself before a magical working, which is something I will cover in more depth later on in this chapter. She may also ground herself, however, when she feels that she has taken on too much negative energy and she needs to get rid of some of it.

In these cases, the act of grounding can be done by itself. And though it might take a fair amount of time when you are first starting out, over time you will find that you can ground and release negative energy in a matter of minutes without much direct thought. You do not have to master grounding this thoroughly before you move on to other meditative tools, of course. But it does help keep you free of negative influences and makes it safer for you to cast spells or do divination on the fly without raising as many protective wards.

The following grounding exercise is an excellent beginning practice. It is designed with earth-based witches in mind. But once you get comfortable with it, you might find that you want to change the stabilizing force that you ground yourself into or the imagery used in your grounding visualizations. If you are just starting out, however, you should stick with the original exercise until you are comfortable with the process.

Before you begin any sort of energy work – which is another term for meditative practices and other ways by which you learn to control your energy – you need to raise your protective wards. When you are first starting out with energy work, you are very vulnerable. Over time you will find that you are less vulnerable when grounded than you are at other times. But at the beginning, opening up your energy like this will leave you vulnerable. So, for now, it is best to do this behind the safety of a protective circle or other similar wards.

Once your wards are raised, you will want to sit in a comfortable position. You can lay down but you run the risk of falling asleep if you try to ground while lying down, at least the first few times. So settle yourself in a comfortable sitting position and close your eyes. When you have gotten comfortable, check in with your body. By this, I mean that you should locate sources of stress and try to release them.

Stress most commonly gathers at the corners of the eyes and across your forehead as well as in your jaw and cheeks. If you find that you are frowning slightly or clenching your jaw, actively work to let go of that stress. From there you can move on to other high-tension areas such as your back or your shoulders. The one place that you want to keep tension, however is in your core. Maintaining good posture is a small form of self-support and self-care that can make meditation of all types much more enjoyable. If you find tension in your core, just make sure that it is serving the purpose of supporting the muscles in your back and maintaining good posture.

You will probably have to check in with your tension levels several times throughout your grounding practice, especially when you are new to the exercise. Trying new things can cause tension, even if only a little bit. So as you work through the grounding process, you should periodically check in and ensure that you are being gentle with yourself as you ground your energy.

After you release all of your unnecessary tension, it is time to begin the actual process of grounding your energy. With your eyes still closed, imagine a thick root emerging from the base of your spine. You can also imagine a network of roots extending down from the places where your body is in contact with the floor, if that makes you more comfortable. Whichever you choose, make sure you bury the roots deep into the soil. Imagine a strong wind trying to knock you over. If the wind fails to move you, even a little bit, the roots are deep enough.

Once you are firmly rooted, turn your attention to your energy. Find a place on your physical body or in your mind where you feel content. If you focus your mental imagery on that area long enough, a specific color will start to form in your mind. This is the color of your energy. When you have this color in mind, turn your attention to the rest of your body and your mind. Look for discolored spots in your energy. You will likely find them in physical places where you feel sick or mental places where negative thoughts dwell. Discolored energy is a sign that negative energy has taken over that location.

Take your time and identify as many spots of discolored energy as you can. Then, starting from the top and working your way down, visualize the discolored spots flowing from their current location down to the roots you sank into the earth. The energy might resist leaving as you push it down through the roots, as negative energy likes to latch onto something and not let it go. But do not give up. Push the energy down the roots over and over until every last bit of it has passed out of your root system and into the earth.

The earth will take this energy and cleanse it, then return the cleansed energy to the universe so that it can be put to fresh use. In this way, negative energies are given a second chance to make a more positive impact in the world.

Once you have released all of that negative energy, you will find that you either feel drained or feel like there are empty spots in your energy field. Addressing this issue is the final step in grounding. After releasing all the negative energy, you can draw fresh neutral energy from a few sources. The most readily available source is the earth that you have rooted yourself into. In addition to cleansing negative energy, the earth stores a lot of neutral potential energy. And this is something you can put to use so that you do not feel so drained and do not have empty spots in your energy field.

Generally speaking, grounding is a very good thing. It can help keep a witch balanced, no matter what they are going through or what spells they are performing. But grounding can also bring up things that people try to ignore in their own minds, particularly when they go to turn out negative energy. If this happens to you, know that it is normal. It is part of what witches call Shadow Work, which is a vital part of any in-depth magical practice. I cover shadow work in greater detail in the last section of this chapter.

Centering

Grounding and centering are usually referenced together. But they are two separate practices with two separate functions. That being said, they *are* complementary and work very well when used together. If you choose to use these processes together you should always ground first, as this will give you a stronger foundation to work from. Once you are rooted, you will have a much easier time controlling where your energy goes. If you choose to center without grounding, however, you just have to make sure that you are careful not to unbalance yourself by releasing or spending too much energy at once.

As with grounding, you will find that you develop your own preferred visualization methods as you get comfortable with the process. To begin with, however, I recommend the visualization that makes up the rest of this section. It is the centering visualization that I started with and it is very simple while being wonderfully effective.

Centering, in general, is the act of evaluating where your energy is going and ensuring that you approve of all your energetic commitments. If you do not, you release some of the commitments as part of the centering process, then center your remaining energy in your core so that you feel more balanced. Before you get to this stage, however, you should raise your wards. Just like with your grounding practice, centering will eventually make you less vulnerable. But at the very beginning, this level of visualization work will open your energy up quite a bit. So make sure you set your wards before you dive into the visualization aspect of centering.

The visualization exercise for this process is very simple. When you did your grounding exercise, you created a mental image of yourself that you used when you formed your energetic roots. You can use that same mental image of yourself for your centering exercise or you can create a new one. If you do choose to use the same mental image as the one you used for your grounding work, you will have to shift the focus up and out so that you can see your whole self at once, rather than just bits and pieces.

When your field of vision contains a mental image of your whole self, slowly spread a sense of awareness out around your body. This sense should reveal all the strands of energy that extend out from you. These strands represent all the energetic commitments you make. Some of these commitments will be obvious, like your connections to friends, family, and your work life. Others may surprise you, such as the level of energy you spend on gossip or worrying about misplacing your phone. We all spend our energy in countless different places. Centering helps us bring some of that energy back home.

Each person views the strands of their energetic commitments differently. For some people, they are just lines the same color as the rest of their energy. These lines might all be the same thickness or they might vary in size depending on the amount of energy that flows down any given connection. Other people see the connections as a different energetic color, since it is not their energy alone but is instead their energy connected with something else.

A third common visual representation of energetic commitments is for each commitment to appear as a different kind of connection. Some may appear as chains, particularly those connections you cannot cut but are not fond of. Others might appear as tinsel, twinkle lights, or ribbons. Each connection will bear its own unique appearance based on the person or thing it is connected to and how you feel about them.

However your connections appear, take your time exploring them. Pay attention to whether or not they look different based on how you feel or if more connections go in one direction than in another. Once you are certain that you have highlighted the vast majority of your energetic connections, begin to go through them one by one. Decide if you are comfortable maintaining those connections. If you are, you also need to make sure that you are comfortable with the level of energy you are putting into them.

When you find connections that you do not want to keep, you have a few options to choose from. The first of these is that you disconnect the energetic connection immediately. Some connections will require real-world or mundane actions to fully sever and you will have to make a mental note to take care of these after you are done centering. But, while you are still engaged in the meditative process, you can cut off the energetic connection as a first step in severing the connection altogether.

If you find several connections that you want to sever, you can gather them into a bundle and go through them all at the same time. You will still have to disconnect them one by one to ensure that you get back as much of your energy as possible. But rather than disconnecting one energy commitment and then refocusing your attention on evaluating the next connection, you can go through all of the connections and then lock your focus in on the process of disconnecting those you no longer need.

Of course, you can also choose to do nothing. But, depending on the connections, this is akin to leaving leeches on your skin. They take from you and give nothing back, leaving you a little weaker with each passing day until you do not have the energy to complete the things that you want to complete. It is best to cut all unwanted and unnecessary connections as soon as possible. But, of course, there are times when it is not possible for one reason or another. In these cases, you can leave the connections in place while putting a throttle on them. This will act as a sort of energy brake so that you do not devote more energy to the connections that is strictly necessary.

Energy throttles are also a good idea for connections that you do want to keep, regardless of how you feel about them. Just because you keep a connection does not mean that you should pour unlimited energy into it. In these cases, an energy throttle can help you maintain a better sense of balance.

When you are ready to disconnect energetic commitments, you need to remember that you are doing so as an act of compassion for yourself rather than an act of punishment for whatever the energy is connected to do. Framing the process in this manner will keep the energy at a neutral or positive level and prevent negative energy from attaching to you or the recently severed connection.

As you break the connection with whoever or whatever your energy was going to, envision the energy rolling back into your core like a tape measure or a length or ribbon being rolled back onto the spool. If you are still grounded, you may want to feed the energy down into the earth and draw up fresh energy to replace it. This is particularly true if the person or thing you were connected to was toxic, whether to you specifically or in a general sense.

When you have gone through all of your energetic connections and sorted those you want from those you do not want, it is time to tend the remaining connections. Energetic connections, like any collection of growing things, needs to be maintained. Nature maintains her own gardens quite well. But when humans become involved, we take the burden of tending these collections on ourselves. And our energetic connections are no different. So take the time in this meditative practice to make sure all your energetic connections are healthy.

Checking the health of your energetic connections is something you should probably do more regularly than you do. Many witches make a point of checking in with these connections on a weekly or monthly basis. This prevents them from running into toxic situations that they are trapped in by pouring too much energy into them. It also ensures that they are not spending more energy than they actually have to give and run themselves ragged, sort of like an energetic budget check.

You might not be ready to commit to such frequent energy checks right away. But you should certainly take the time to go through them all the first time you center. Healthy energetic bonds should be a strong, pleasing color. The exact color and appearance may vary, as I already said. But it should be pleasing to you, since it is your energy being expended. It should also look healthy without any breaks, cracks, or splinters. Finally, healthy energetic connections will not leave your feeling drained. You can adore the person or thing on the other end of an energetic connection. But if you are exhausted due to your connection with them, there is an imbalance you must correct.

Once you have done all of this, gather your energetic bonds into one hand and focus them in your core. This will give them a strong foundation to draw from and help you keep a better eye on them, as they are all rooted in a place you can easily reach. At this point you can close out the visualization and return to the mundane world.

If you found any connections that you want to sever and doing so requires real-world action, now is the time to take them. Putting off the necessary real-world actions opens you up to a new energetic connection that you then have to go back in and sever again.

As with grounding, centering may pull up connections and energetic expenditures that force you to look at things or connections you do not want to. If this happens, it may be a sign that you are ready for Shadow Work. Shadow Work is a very intense form of self-reflection and magic use, however. If you feel called to it, be sure and commune with your chosen higher power or the spirits that you work with before divine into it. You will likely find that you need their support as you explore the depth of the shadows, as I discuss in the final section of this chapter.

Meditation and Visualization in Spellwork and Magic

Earlier in this chapter I touched on the fact that meditation and visualization can help in your magical workings. In fact, many of the spells in my other books rely on visualization to focus the energy of the spell. A few are reliant solely on visualization. But you do not have to cast a spell for meditation to be useful in your magical practice. In fact, there are several ways that this skill can come in handy for all manner of witches and magic users.

The most obvious benefit of visualization is that it can help you work through tangled thoughts and confusing signals. Although this is something that everyone could benefit from, magic users will find it particularly useful. Our magic is controlled in large part by our feelings and our intentions. Although it is not quite as dramatic as it appears in movies and on TV, the connection between a witch's state of mind and their magic is very real.

You might not lose control and level an entire office building or something like that. But if you are in a negative state of mind – or if you are suffering from a lot of confusion and conflicting thoughts – you might find it hard, or even impossible, to properly control your energy. You will still be able to use charged objects. And you can probably raise your wards without too much trouble. But casting spells or calling spirits you are not closely linked to will be nearly impossible. And the longer it goes on, the harder it will be, which only creates a negative feedback loop.

When you find yourself feeling conflicted or frustrated, meditation can help. If you are too tangled up to use your usual divination method, meditation is a great way to connect more directly with your guiding forces and with yourself. Should you succeed with other forms of divination but struggle to interpret the answers you received, meditation can help you figure out the information your guides are trying to show you.

Meditation is not strictly for the times when you are feeling down and out, however. You can also use meditation and mindfulness to help you choose the right spell for any given situation. Or, if you feel that you are ready to write your own spells, meditating on your goal and the other spells you have seen will help you connect dots you might have otherwise not noticed.

Finally, meditating is a great way to let your higher power or your spiritual guides reach you without opening yourself up to too much outside energy. This is particularly true if you try to meditate while seated with a protective circle. Although many meditation practices encourage you to completely empty your mind, meditating to connect with your guiding forces works a little bit differently. Rather than trying to keep a completely blank mind, focus your thoughts on the particular guiding force you want to connect with. Then follow where they seem to nudge your mind.

This will take some practice. At first, you will probably chastise yourself because you feel that you are getting off-task or that your mind is going down paths that your guides couldn't possibly mean for you to go down. But over time, as you strengthen your connection with your higher power or spiritual guides as well as your sense of discernment, you can trust the direction of your mind during these meditation sessions more fully. For the time being, remember to talk to yourself with compassion when you meditate with your guiding forces. It is the best way to notice all the cues your guides are sending you.

Of course, you may find that you want to meditate for non-magical reasons. After all, not everything you do has to focus on your magical practice, though many witches try to incorporate their magical side as fully into their daily lives as possible. If you are of the mind that you want to spend time with your thoughts for non-magical reasons, you need only raise a protective ward and set your intentions. If a guiding force tries to get your attention, gently state that you are not open to magical urging at the moment and are instead focused on organizing your thoughts or finding some calm. If they are a truly positive entity – and it is not an emergency – they will respect the boundary you have set.

Shadow Work

It seems fitting to end this chapter and this book with a section on Shadow Work. Not because Shadow Work is an ending. But because delving into this aspect of magic is something that should only be attempted by those who are comfortable with both their practices and their control of their own energy. And though I refer to it in several places as a process, make no mistake that Shadow Work is a tool. It is something that helps you know yourself more fully and, be extension, work your magic with more confidence.

Although Shadow Work is something that should be performed by experienced magic workers, it is such an important tool that I wanted to cover it in this book. If you find that it appeals to you – and you are ready – please consider this as a foundation on which to build your understanding of Shadow Work and the ways it can improve not only your magical life and the connections it creates but your mundane life and all that it touches on as well.

Shadow Work is the act of looking at the things that hide in the shadows of our minds and the shadowy depths of our energetic connections. Despite the name, this is not an act performed in darkness. And the process itself is anything but dark. In order to find that which lives in the shadows we contain, we must shine light on them To do that, we must carry the light within ourselves, just as we carry the darkness.

Everyone has shadows. If people seem that they have no shadows at all, it either means that they are very good at hiding them or it means that their shadows are much, much deeper than you would expect. No matter how happy a person seems, *everyone* has shadows within themselves. It takes a very strong person to sit down with the parts of themselves that thrive in this darkness and try to come to an understanding. Such strength is, unfortunately, hard to develop and often quite rare. Because of this, many people go their whole lives without fully understanding the way they work or why certain things affect them the way they do.

As a witch, you do not have the luxury of living in this way. The more magic you do, the more in touch with your own energy you are. You *will* notice the energy drains and you will eventually have to confront the things taking your energy. Yes, you need to know how to control your energy before you dive into Shadow Work. And, for a time, you will still be new enough to the world of magic that you will not know what to look for in terms of spotting cues that your shadows are encroaching on your magical energy.

But as you gain more experience and more awareness of yourself, you will see more and more places where your shadows interfere with your magical life. When this happens, it is time to sit down with your higher power or spiritual guides and determine where it is they want you to begin. You can perform shadow work without guidance from a higher power. Secular witches do it all the time. But if you generally work with a higher power or spiritual guides, your self-exploration will be better served if you carry it out with their help.

It should be noted that, if you were a very self-aware person prior to starting your magical practice, you may be called to Shadow Work much sooner than other witches who are at your level of experience. You will have to make the choice of whether or not you are going to answer the call now or if you wait. In order to make this choice, you need to honestly evaluate your abilities in a few areas.

Successful Shadow Work reveals a lot about the witch who is carrying it out without disrupting their ability to live their life. On the contrary, diving into the depth of their shadows should bring their daily life a little more balanced because they can face themselves more fully. Until they do this, certain things will throw off the rhythm of their life, in much the same way as missing a step going up a flight of stairs will. For a moment your feet do not know where to go and your sense of balance is off as adrenaline spikes in your system. Living while you only know part of yourself is much like that. Shadow Work seeks to correct this imbalance.

There are a few ways that you will know you have been called to Shadow Work. Many of them will only become obvious when you create your own understanding of signs and portents. For some witches, it is the sudden and frequent appearance of certain animals. Ravens and wolves are common motifs, particularly for those that follow the Norse pantheon. This is because Odin is not just a god of wisdom but also journeying, magic, and discovery. Seeing animals with connections to him are usually signs he wants your attention.

Other similar gods are Hades, who rules the underworld which is a land of shadows and things forgotten, as well as his wife Persephone. Many are surprised to learn that Persephone is a goddess who encourages Shadow Work. But she is also a goddess who chose to walk in the shadows of the Underworld when she could have remained in the light. It is not hard to see why she would be someone who encourages others to do the same.

As you can see, none of these gods are inherently negative. And despite the fact that many negative things live in our shadows, Shadow Work is quite possibly the most positive think you can do for yourself. Not only will you face those things that you might have wanted to bury and not properly deal with, but you might also discover buried hopes and dreams that you thought had long since vanished. Through Shadow Work, you can bring them back to the surface and help make them into a reality if they still appeal to you.

Another way that you might receive the nudge to begin Shadow Work is through your dreams. Earlier in this chapter I talked about how you can use dreams as a form of divination, but that you have to be careful not to enter into lucid dreaming unintentionally. Witches occasionally find themselves lucid dreaming with absolutely no effort on their part. When this happens, a visit from a spiritual guide or higher power is usually not far behind. So long as the spirit does not set off any warning bells – again, this is a time when discernment is very important – that visit will likely begin your Shadow Work journey.

Shadow Work largely consists of meditation practices, journaling, and spells that encourage self-reflection. As I said before, it is a very large and deeply personal process. But if you feel called to it – and you have checked with your higher power to ensure that is the direction you should go – the first few steps are simple enough.

To begin your Shadow Work journey, you will need a journal I strongly encourage you to keep your Shadow Work journal separate from the rest of your grimoire. Shadow Work is part of your magical journey, yes. But it is involved enough that you will want more room to explore the ideas and revelations your

Shadow Work generates. To this end, a separate and dedicated journal is a good way to ensure you have enough room. And, if you find that your magical workings are changing as you progress with your Shadow Work, you can cross reference your Shadow Work journal with your grimoire.

Shadow Work may seem intimidating, and it should. It should not, however, be frightening. Yes, it will bring things into the light that might be uncomfortable. But it does not change who you are. Rather, it helps you understand who you are on a more fundamental level. Shadow Work creates stronger connections between you, your energy, and your magical self. And this will only make you stronger on every front.

When it is time, you will know. Shadow Work is not something to be rushed and it is not something to be jumped into without proper preparation. A journal is only one part of the tools you need to fully engage in Shadow Work. A full set of psychic armor and the ability to repair it are also paramount. A strong connection to a set of divination tools is also recommended. These will help you get back on the path you are meant to take whenever you feel that you are slipping into territory that makes no sense. And, of course, you need a strong connection to your higher power or your guides. They will guide you and protect you as you master Shadow Work, the most intangible and yet one of the most powerful tools any witch can possess.

Conclusion

Thank you for making it through to the end of *Witchcraft Supplies: A Guide for Solitary Practitioners to the Tools a Witch Needs for Her Rituals and Spells*. It is my sincere wish that it helped you find the answers you were looking for. And that it illuminated new steps on your path through the amazing world of magic.

If you liked this book and want to continue with me on this journey, please consider a few of my other books. *The Beginner Witch* covers many basic aspects of magic and will help set the foundation for a strong and well-informed magical practice. *Modern Witchcraft for Beginners* takes the usual expectations about magical practices and turns them on their ear. It showcases how technology and magic can not only work together but complement each other while providing examples of ways that old practices can be adapted to fit a modern life. And *Herbal Witchcraft* is a kitchen witch's best friend. It will tell you everything you need to know about basic kitchen witchery and herbal studies.

Finally, if you found this book useful in any way, a review on Amazon is always appreciated!

Made in the USA
Monee, IL
23 October 2020